AF364279

RICO CORTEZ DUKES

ULTIMATE FAMILY BETRAYAL

BETRAYAL

ISBN: 9788832542714

This ebook was created with StreetLib Write
http://write.streetlib.com

CREDITS

I like to thank my cousin GEORGE CALVIN LEE FOR LOVING ME ENOUGH TO GO AGAINST THE POWERS THAT BE FOR THE LOVE OF HIS FAMILY WHICH ULTIMATE COST HIM HIS LIFE I WOULD FOREVER LOVE YOU TILL THE END...LOVE YOU AND YOUR WORDS ARE NEVER FORGOTTEN ...I LOVE YOU GEORGE CALVIN LEE RIH.....

THE BIRTH OF A LEADER

THE BIRTH

ON AUGUST 26,1979 In Shreveport Louisiana Rico Cortez Dukes was born to Father Robert Charles Dukes and,Mother Teretha Merritt at Doctors hospital at 5:18 am.Born 7pd 8oz was a handsome baby boy that would soon one day become the voice and, leader of the people.Growing up in the small but, deadly hood of Cedar Grove taught Rico the ins and,outs of both, the good and the bad about the aspects of life. At the age of 11 while living in Hollywood in Shreveport Rico and a few other boys was riding there bikes when one of the boys was struck by a truck, that later died, from his injuries.Channel 12 news arrived at the scene which was on Vivian street, News 12 interviewed two of the boys while at the scene Rico spoke not a word while watching the boy fight to breath from his injuries he sustained.News 12 interviewed 2 of the boys without the consent of their parents Rico went home to find out his father had seen the news. And seen his son was at that scene thinking his father,would be upset Rico spoke not a word,his father spoke first.His father seen the deep look on his son face and said son what happened,Rico looked at his father for a few moments and then spoke.Telling his father what he wouldn't say to Channel 12 news..Rico told his dad that the boy who was hit by the truck was chased by a another lil boy who came off another street two streets from Vivian street.The look the lil boy had on his face when seeing the other boy was a look of complete fear on his face that the lil boy feared for his life..Telling his dad that the lil boy took off so fast trying to escape, he never even looked as he went across the street where the speeding truck awaited.As the truck hit the child Rico and the other boys jammed on their brakes,the lil boy pursuing the boy, that was hit kept on riding leaving Rico and the other boys left to watch the lil boy fighting for his life..As a child baseball and football was my favorite sports I played little league baseball for the Cedar Grove Wildcats and football for Cedar Grove Tigers.The baseball team won many championships while the football team learn to lose only winning two games that year..By the time i was 13 i was a star, football player free safety at Bethune Middle School. Even though we only won two games that season my guess was, two was the lucky number for those years! I later went on to attend Byrd High School,Where my grades were good but,my fighting lead to suspensions and my father soon sent me to another school.Not knowing That Fair Park High School at that time was real gang related and was only more trouble for Me.First day at Fair park high i had a fight with one of the rival blood gang members from Queens Borough QB. Myself and the guy was suspended for nine days while on my suspension my little sister introduced me to her boyfriend Albert Battson aka Pig. Myself,and pig became like real brothers, that would die for each other.While i had a little cousin who was like my little brother George Calvin Lee.Pig introduced me and my cousin George to this fellow name Trigger Myron Gipson,it was 4 of me Pig Trigger and George.. Trigger well,the name tells it all,While i was the quiet deadly silent one. George was the one who many thought was just a quiet teenager not knowing the gangsta bloodline within him.Pig, well, he was the less understanding one who many knew, meant business the 4 of us became a force to be reckoned.At age 17 I was stabbed in the face in my hood at age 19 I caught my first drug case and was sentenced to two years and sent to Franklin Correctional Center 179 miles away from Shreveport. Doing my sentence time, my father had a massive heart attack but God seen my father through .I remember telling my father not to die on me while I was locked up his reply, with his deep southern voice I'm not gone die on you Co.I was released in 2001 and went straight back to the streets of drug dealing which was why I was locked up in the first place.But as we know sometimes one must bump his head hard enough to leave a knot to change I was one that had to..I'm now 21 and home from my jail stay back united with my crew which had it hard with me being away.I reorganized my crew stronger then we was before I left I had two years to think about how to and, I did so.At this time one of my close friends had stepped up major while I was away Johnny Johnson (Boosie B) now I had other connections but me in Boosie was childhood friends .He was apart of the 4 but he was unseen to many which made us five in total but only 4 was seen.. Boosie was a slick one, very quite, very humble, and very smart but slick never the less.I went to my dad's house a little after I was out myself,and Boosie my little sister was home at the time,I went to see my pops.My sister seen Boosie and she couldn't stop smiling now Boosie was a light bright complexion dude about 5 feet 11 he was about 210 in weight with thin line facial hair who was a school boy that managed the fast money well which his why he was needed in the click.I introduced my sister and Boosie and they went from there with there conversation I went into my pops room his face lit up like a child at Christmas upon seeing his baby boy free.I talked to my pops for a while now it was time to roll out and take care of other things .I met my first child mother Sheria foster when I was 16 and she was 15 we had my first child and Sheria second child one year later Dominique Foster.Sheria Foster and I was in a relationship for 10 years but we continued to see each other until our mid 30s.At the time of me being locked up we was still together while I was locked up she got engaged to be married.Sheria stood about 5'0 feet dark skin long black natural hair with a body shape that most older woman couldn't compare to at that time in other words she was bad.All the older men wanted her I remember seeing her and said damn I got to have her and I did for many many years.My daughter was my heart my first child the joy I so much needed she was born January 3 1997 a beautiful baby girl.I was doing a few days in jail for a misdemeanor charge when Sheria went into labor my daughter didn't arrive till after I was released my baby waited on her dad to be free at least that was my thought!!After my daughter I applied myself full time to the streets of hustling I knew I had a mouth to feed so the streets was the fastest way but not the best way.As I mentioned about the four to be reckoned with myself,Trigger,pig and George.We set up shop in a neighborhood called Ingleside a very small hood but the money was very good to be such a small hood. We had a few competitions that was around before we set up shop but our presence was soon very well known and money became bigger and better that a few didn't like but they soon was on our boat in one way are the other.The first Street where shop was set up was Desoto street at My cousin Tavara Lee house who was George sister it was across the street from a competitor that was in that hood before us well at least some ways.I remember many days getting calls from the competitor telling me that Trigger was taken they clients telling me trigger was calling their clients out of their yard.On this one day they called in told me please get to my spot cause trig was tripping out I didn't know how but,i knew I had to get there because I knew trig and so did they.I get there and trig in our spot yard with the 25 caliber telling them they can't come out they yard and he was telling their clients to come over but,the crazy thing was they was letting him do it ... I knew at that point they feared trig so I instructed trig to stand down from terrorizing them and told him we don't need the police called on us because the competitor was afraid.The competitor Thanked me for that I still laugh about all that and wondering how did they allow trig to do that but,i know how they was afraid being afraid and trying to be a drug dealer don't go hand and hand.Never the less many ignore the hand and hand advice and find themselves being took advantage of because of the fear they have.Lets Fast forward back to 21 years old and being released as I said my crew was back stronger then we was before we had many spots through out Ingleside.One spot we had did so many numbers many thought we was getting a kilo are two at that time.Thanks to a homie it was shut down from a shooting that was behind my homie now he decides he wanted to jump on his baby mother in front of her dad he beat her all the way out her shirt.He come to our spot right after which was about four houses down from the spot telling me and trig he was about to go talk to her dad we told him not to go but,he went anyway.He could not have been down there five minutes before myself and trig heard shots we ran to the front door my homie running and holding his chest hollering I'm shot I'm shot and screaming for someone to shoot.As I'm standing in the door way I hear bullets hitting my spot but my homie was in the line of fire I'm screaming telling him to fall so shots can be fired back.He heard me just in time before the old man took aim to finish him just as my homie fell shots rang out from our end in the pitch black dark 29 shots was fired, ending the shooting from the other end of the street.The shooting left two people shot my homie was shot in his leg with a 357 Magnum and his baby mother was hit four times my homie went to jail for aggravated assault for that shooting the laws ask him who was shooting by Stander's told them Rico shot him. He came from under the oxygen mask and told the police my home boy didn't shoot me my bby mommy daddy did they asked him who shot your bby mommy he put the oxygen mask back on so,the laws told him he was being charged for the shooting .The next day I go to the spot to get a few things my baby mother Sheria pulls up I tell her to leave because it was a shoot out last night she left but told me to come to her house.My homie got 5 years for the shooting to this day I still wonder why was he holding his chest but was shot in the leg.Months before that my homie mommy house was shot up by rivals from the Cooper Road which is where my homie Mike was from.I was told that shooting was behind Mike as well After all that we relocated on the other side of ingleside on Drexel street once again money was good. But for some reason things started to change with trig even though he was always a dont trust type of nigga which my lil bro pig told me BUT PIG was the one who introduced me to trig.Product came up missing and 8 guns two 9mm flocks both 15 shot one 10 shot 40 cab a 32 revolver two 25 and few others myself an George was gone when all this occurred trig claim he left to but it would soon come clear what was really taking place.George and I started putting the puzzle together and it was pointing to trig but why ,what is true motive? Few days pass and the true motive started to reveal me and George had words with trig on some shit he brought up to us but his whole attention was to create this fairy tell lie to strike the argument that he wanted to lead to other things and it did! Him knowing us and knowing we wasn't gone stand for the shit he was talking which is why he hid all the guns in the first place.It soon lead to trig running to go get the 40 cab he stole and hid from us. George wanted to kill him that night I told my lil cuz we need to get all our guns first but ,then I told him we gone get the guns cut his supply of and let him starve and he did.You see trig is Calvin Reed first cousin two sisters children I will get into who Calvin Reed is a little later.Now let's pause for a minute so I can fill you in on a few things first thing his a female by the name of Shunting Goines and her family .Shuntina was someone I used to talk to in middle school but later in life we hooked it back up.I will fill you in about her in the government plot chapter.My life is not a average life it consists of hurt deep BETRAYAL and government Secrets this book gives my readers a full understanding of how and why I'm who I am and my whole movement at hand.How can someone please if they only wish to care about just their to lead one must accept criticism one must accept to fail in order to be great one must understand only mistakes make greatness without making mistakes how can one find there on flaws.Most important every great leader must be willing to understand and know that the cause he are she stands for is greater then one own family.In order to love one must first learn to forgive and in order to forgive one must learn how to heal from the hurt that is within ..A person can not love if they are still holding on the pain that cause them to stop Loving.Love is the only key to unity and unity is the key to success your unity starts with the most high God YAH-WEH..

CHILDHOOD AND TEENAGE YEARS

Growing up

Born and raised in Cedar Grove a small but deadly hood in Shreveport Louisiana he learn the good and bad at 18 he moved to other parts of the city and took his lesson with him on a journey that awaited him he never imagined.Growing up in cedar Grove not a easy task,but it taught me a lot of life lessons about the ins and outs of life the good and the bad.I was 16 when my mom told me to choose my friends and the streets are home I chose the streets i told her that I would never live with her again in life and from 16 to 39 I held my end of that deal.At the age of 16 I was in the streets heavy Damon Porter was my best friend us two did a lot and I had another childhood friend named Johnny Johnson BOOSIE B and Jew man.T his chapter will give you a look into my childhood of friends and some kids mothers I was always a very outspoken person and straight forward.. Me BOOSIE and DAMON were real close growing up some said we was family me and BOOSIE have the same niece Alyssa Merritt my sister his her mother and BOOSIE brother Calvin Johnson is her Father.One night me and DAMON was standing on 74th which is the street i lived on with my mom Teretha MERRITT damon tells me he was about to go home we both seen a car sitting on the side of the road but we couldn't make out what kind of car so DAMON said he would check it out as he got closer as he gets closer to the car he holler and tells me it Duchie I said fuck because I didn't have my pistol with me on the corner it was at the house in the bushes three houses from the corner.Now let me explain who lil duchie was he was a fighter a shooter and a Killa who had murdered many people in his time.The reason we was beefing was because he set me up to be robbed at his uncle tick tock house on East 76th street.The crazy part was half the drugs was his that I was robbed for..At this time duchie was giving me fronts a half ounce of coke and Herbert Cheek's was fronting me a half as well me and duchie took turns working the east and west side of our hood Cedar Grove.We rotated every other day. Duchie pull up to pick me up so he feels the need to show me his money and said you see all the money I'm making when we split up.I laughed and pulled mines out and said you see all the money I be making when we split up but my bank was bigger he knew nothing about the other connect I had.He tells me how you made all that money I laughed and gave him his 375 dollars and said the same way you do the look in his eye when he asked me that should have told me something.Instead I ignored the look and continue the conversation him he finally said you want to work the east I said yes. We go to his uncle tick tock house he drops me off and leave had 30 mins after he left two guys walk up one being bay boy the other Earl now I didn't know who Earl was at that time but I knew who bay boy was from his older brother shitty me in shitty was cool but I had never really seen bay boy until this day I was robbed.. Earl ask for double up for 40 dollars I go to look in the bag to get it and see a metal object out the corner of my eye it wasn't a gun but to this day I still have no clue what it was but it left me swoll over the left side of my eye and the side of my head..He hit me multiple times I remember him trying to get the dope out my hand at some point he succeeded in doing so..Earl runs off and bay boy steps up as if he didn't know it was about to happen asking me I'm I OK and helping me sit up then he say that's fucked up I didn't know he was bout to do that knowing the whole time duchie sent them.Bay boy tell me he bout to go see if he can find the guy and he leaves a little while later duchie pulls up saying he heard what happened but how no one was out that morning and his uncle was sleep.But I tell him anyway and he tells me he still want his money knowing he sent them.I knew right then it was gone be beef cause I wasn't pay-ing him I get to my house and I'm running it with damon about it Duchie used to talk to Damon sis-ter damon his who introduced me to Duchie.Da-mon tells me duchie sent them at me..Time passes as I said earlier me in Damon standing on 74 duchie parked down the streets with his lights off but he to far to be seen just right off..When me in Damon look and finally see the car we ask each other is that a car sitting with its park lights on DAMON tell me he bout to go home and he will see who the car is are what it is.As he gets closer to the car he holler and tell me that's duchie I said fuck and duchie smashed on the gas coming for me I broke out running to try in get to my gun that was in the bushes of my yard duchie car was to fast! I had to run pass the bushes because he was already there.I ran to the back yard into the outside shed that was in the back yard..I hear leaves ruffling in the alley behind the house I knew it wasn't duchie because he was paralyzed so I knew it was one of his henchman I hear a whistle coming from the front of the house it's duchie signaling his henchman to come on.I hear the henchman leave because I hear the leaves just as I heard them when he came only this time the sound is going instead of coming.I wait a few minutes before I go out to make sure the coast his clear I hear one door close I know the henchman just got in the car.By this time I'm out the shed and hear duchie yell I'm get you pussy I ease to the bushes and retrieve my gun I so just needed but was unable to reach it when needed.I told myself that night never to leave ANYWHERE WITHOUT MY PISTOL..Now I got to deal with cheeks so I call him over to let him know what happened and to give him most of his money.He pulls up in his maroon Chevy Heartbeat truck I'm stand outside

when he pulls up damon sitting on my porch under the car porch with the gun I got my gun on
my side.I walk out to his truck and tell him what's
up and give him 800 of the 1200 dollars I owe him
and tell him I will have the rest on Friday which
was always the original day to pay this was a
Wednesday pulled up so I'm still on schedule.I
guess he was drunk well I know he was it was very
rare he wasnt drinking this night he was already
almost to his max.He tells me I know what happened is true because I heard about it I understand but I need all mine. I'm thinking I just told
you the rest still gone be on schedule for Friday as
always so I told him exactly what I was thinking I
don't know if I should have said it differently do to
the fact of the circumstances are if he should have
not been so drunk to not hear it clear but either
way I stated what I thought and said in my mind
and what I had said already.He replied like I said
nigga u gone pay me are its gone be something before I knew it the outspoken savage came out and
I said nigga get it in blood since you talking like
that and I just told you the rest still will be on Friday I told now it's what ever and it was..He peeled
rubber from in front of my mom's house and the
weeks later we seen each other at the liquor store

he's in the drive thru.Its me my cousin poppa
which is Edward Richardson and Jew man and
DAMON me in Jew man in the back of the truck
and Jew tells me there go cheeks get down I tell
jew man fuck that I'm not getting down.I hop out
the truck forgetting my pistol with my cousin
bebe poppa older brother.Cheeks see me and say
what's up nigga I look at him and walk to his truck
he was counting money in his hand his I got to the
driver side of the heart beat truck Window and
seen the chrome 9 with the beam sitting on the
passenger seat.we talked for a brief second then
he reached and grabbed the 9mm that was on the
seat next to him.I thought of him pulling the trigger in my face God made him put it between his
legs and continue counting the money he was
counting when we pulled in.He went to talking
crazy again and I replied fuck it at that time he
reached for the 9mm I started to back away from
the truck i turn around I hear his truck door starting to open.I take off running my cousin poppa
see what's going on as I pass the truck i hit the
back end of the truck to tell my cousin to hit it
popped smashed into reverse just as cheeks was
shot the bullet hit the very back end of the truck
that I had just tapped telling him to hit it.I ran to

73 street then got a ride to get my pistol.Later that night I waited for hours for cheeks to come home across the street from his house he finally made it home and shots was fired .He didn't come home that night are at least the hours I waited for him. Months later bebe had the beef quashed with cheeks and me and DAMON had the beef quashed between me and duchie right before DAMON was gunned down.Duchie was killed in 1998 by police and cheeks died in a motorcycle crash this all happened in a three year span.The block I grew up on West 77th I seen many things that a young person shouldn't see.I realized I didn't want to be like all the others from my hood I wanted my voice to be heard by the world but never knowing years later I would be a Civil rights leader for the people that have been so mislead by the illegal American system.After damon was killed I moved about 6 months later never telling his mom are sister why are even letting them know i was I just left one day and never returned.It was to much on me to stay at that house and my best friend was gone.His mom and sister finally called me a few days later because they hadn't seen are heard from me I told them I left cause I quit my job.But, I think they truly knew why I left I remember his sister Lou

telling me we miss me to Rico and we love you and you can come home anytime you ready tears rolled down my face hearing those words.Many years later while in my 30 damon mom was in the nursing home where my ex wife worked who was my wife at that time.Shirley called me and told me that she takes care of this sweet old lady who has Alzheimer's and said she asked her did she have any kids.She said the lady named Ms Porter told me she had five kids a daughter and four sons she asked what her son's name was and the lady said moomoo damon Rico and lil John she said ms Porter eyes watered up when she said Damon dead now and RICO I haven't seen in years.Shirley said she asked her what was Rico last name and she said his last name is Dukes she told her Rico is my husband she said you want me to call him so he can come see you she said yes but she didn't think he would come shirley called me in told me everything that was said I couldn't stop the tears from falling.I stopped and turned around and flew to that nursing home to see my mother the woman who took me in when my real mother put me out .I walked into the nursing room she was in she looked up at me and tears fell from hear eyes when she seen me she said my baby I walked up to her and gave her a hug so tight while she cried and told me how much she missed me but didn't know where I was.We talked for a while before I left.I left instructions with my ex wife to make sure she take care of her and told mommy to let me know if she need anything at all to let me know a little while later maybe couple months mommy passed.

THE GOVERNMENT MURDER PLOT

Plot

NoOn November 26, 2010 i was shot nine times leaving 23 total,gunshot holes in me from a GOVERNMENT murder hit. That,revealed a truth that, could not be found without the MOST HIGH GOD YAHWEH to reveal it.November 26,2010 Rico Dukes died that night,upon his awakening, a King and, leader was born....From 22 till bout 33 money was coming in like clock work high way trips Cartel connections and all.I got to start this chapter,of my life with the crosses,that was put in play from who and,the lies of why.Year 1997 was the first attempt on my life from the government hit when I was stabbed in the face but, never knowing that it was a government hit! Micheal Morgan did the stabbing but I did the whooping ass that night, on West 77th street even though, I was stabbed in the face.On this particular night,Damon Porter,nor Boosie, two very close friends at that time went to the block that night we all was pose to go BUT, FOR SOME REASON THEY TOLD ME, TO GO AND THEY WOULD COME LATER.I went as planned,Damon mother was a EASTERN STAR and,she told me not to go because something was gone happen to me never the less I went failing to listen to the warning at hand, knowing all I know now, I understand how in why she told me that.I was not on the block 30 minutes before this very strange incident oc-curred, it was about 9:30 pm that night,me and four others was in the yard, and we just out like al-ways and Michael Morgan who, never was on the block, was out there.He went to talking crazy, no one knew who are, what he was talking about so no one paid him any attention, we figured he was just drunk in high!..But, as he's talking, he decided to throw a full beer directly by my feet, with the beer from the broken glass getting on me,because he was standing right by me, and he stated who- ever don't like it, do something about it.At this time, I looked around at the others, then I glanced down at the broken glass and beer, and said, nigga you must be talking to me .He went to walk around a car, that was backed in the drive way, me not knowing, that was the time he needed to get the knife out his pocket.As he was coming around the car, I met him at the back end of the car on the passenger side,because he went around the car from the driver side.When we met, he swong first stabbing me in the face, across the nose where the bone, of the nose stop.At that time, I thought he had just swong, because it was dark as hell never knowing I was stabbed at this time. I hit him, three four times he grabbed me as I bent my head down, to well on him blood shot out the opened stab wound.I slammed him to the ground, in my mind I'm thinking when he swong he bust my nose, until I seen the six inch blade, in his hand from the glare of the street light, that reflected off the chrome blade.Now im very pissed knowing he stabbed me, I started to hit him with fist, ,knees ,elbows while holding the hand he had the knife in, as I'm hitting him im calling for the others,to help get the knife out his hand but, any effort was useless.They tried,but to no success I'm losing grip on his hand that the knife in,because all the blood I was losing! I took matters into my own hand when I realized the blade of the knife had unlocked to fold down from the pressure of our hands. So I folded the blade down, slicing through his finger down to the bone.He let out a whale of screams,, from the blade slicing through his finger like hot butter, but he still didn't release the knife even, with the blade cut to his bone on his pointer finger.Those out there,, was trying to break us apart, so we got back on our feet now at this time, I know it's all are nothing, I hit him with elbows, fist, knees he called out y'all get him off me, and was telling me please stop, he wasn't gone stab me anymore! But, I heard nothing, and continue to apply very effective fist,elbows,and knees until two people got between us .I'm standing in the yard bloody, from head to toe ,i look at him with blood still running down my face and cheeks, I reached on my side for my 25 caliber, and it wasn't there forgetting Boosie had asked for it right before I left !!BUT WHY? BOOSIE AND DA-MON, NEVER CAME TO THE BLOCK, I walked home to 73 street, where me and DAMON stayed with his mom and sister LOUCHINA PORTER. Boosie and Damon, was pulling up saying they just left the block,and people on the block told them what happened.Boosie, was the one with the car at that time so Boosie, and Damon,drove me to LSU Hospital now, called University Health hospital.I had to have, 17 snitches to close up the stab wound in my nose..Remember Shuntina Goines, I talked shortly about her, in chapter one now,less discuss her now me and Shuntina Goines had sex once AND A RUBBER WAS USED. ANYWAY, MONTHS LATER, I stopped by her house, and she was outside as we talking,she tell me she was pregnant. I'm like OK congrats, knowing we used a condom, she tell me it's mine! Im like huh, what, how, we used a rubber, she tell me I know but, she crying so I'm asking her why she crying. I ask her how is it mines, if we used a rubber, she told me it must have broke. I told her how, when she watched me take it off, and it was in a whole rubber then she said I know Rico, it must had a pin hole in it.At this time, I started to laugh she said Rico you the only one, I been with I said I couldn't have she crying up a storm now, I'm trying to figure out, why she crying so I ask her why she crying like that.She tells me the doctor told her SHE HAS HIV now I'm like huh, what,so she tell me her uncle that's in Angola pissed off and,her daddy. I asked her who is her uncle she never told me.I asked her so they think I gave it to you she told me yes I told them.I told her so you got them thinking I did that shit by this time her daddy pulling up in they hard he look and see me I wanted to talk to him but she said Rico just go I don't want nothing to happen.I refused but she begged me so I left ..I run this to Boosie he tells me her uncle is JOHNNY CAPERS A NOTORI-OUS KILLIER WHO HAS LIFE FOR A STRING OF MURDERS I told Boosie what that mean I didn't give her SHIT HE tells me but Rico he can still make moves he got people out here.I replied,and what that mean.Years pass I have kids none with NOTHING WRONG WITH THEM she has four kids total now.In 2008 my cousin Tavara call me in tell me that some guys in a blue round body Chevy with Texas tags came looking for me and she haven't ever seen them before and neither did I know, mind you this 10 years later are more then ten years.Few months later I get a blocked phone call saying you riding around in that red Cadillac passing that shit out I'm bout to make your life a living hell told me that red girl you fucked was the wrong one.I'm heated now not knowing what the fuck was going on.But still never thinking about 10 12 years before at this time I have 7 kids. One of my son's mother Shatory Washington,told me she was gone kill me and get away with it, January 3 2009 this same baby mother stabbed me in the groin.And never was charged in 2008 my first child called me one early morning crying woke me up out my sleep. I asked her what's wrong she told me daddy I had a dream and it felt so real. She said daddy you was at IN n OUT store and you was going to get some gas and a dude seen you and asked did you have some weed and you said no.She said daddy you went paid for your gas then as you was walking to pump my gas she said daddy he gunned you down then she broke down crying harder.I told her stop crying I'm here baby it was a dream she said daddy it felt to real.I asked her in your dream who told you I was at the store shot she said someone who was at the store that knew me and knew Tavara and knew that me in Tavara was cousins she said they called Tavara and Tavara called in told her mom what happened.That dream my lil girl told me stayed with me for awhile.I slowed down because my daughter made me promise her that I would I did for bout a year are close to a year.One day maybe bout a year later my daughter mommy Sheria foster asked me was I into it with the government I told her no and asked what was she talking bout she replied I'm just asking co and asked me was I sure that I had not did nothing to the government I told her no she asked was I sure again I told her yes because it was the truth.She just looked at me with fear in her eyes but never saying why she asked those questions.Now Trigger knew about it all which is why he did the things he did that I mentioned in chapter 1. By this time things getting crazy and I'm trying to put the pieces together but was missing some major pieces that those close to me held but fell to tell me what was going on.How do you love someone and know there life in danger but tell them nothing when you know what is going on so to me that person is apart of the plot.George told all kind of lies on me to fulfill his part in this secret society government hit plot Everytime he went to jail his dad and sister said it was my fault no matter what he went to jail for they blamed me 95 percent of the time i was no where around when he went to jail.George was about 6 feet 1 200 plus pounds dark skinned low hair cut thick mustache and goatee major car person one who loved to fix them up trade them sell them are keep them.The lies he told was that I was a snitch and got him jammed up he was the flashy type but took a lot of fronts to keep up with the Jones.His sister Tavara turned him against me because she was working with the government in the plot against me.Tavara me and George was very close at one time until,Tavara decided to work for the government.She started working for them back when she caught her food stamp fraud case but the plot had been up against me I just started catching on to her around her food stamp fraud case but never taught she was going against me.See the GOVERNMENT knew it was gone take someone close to me that knew my moves and knew certain people I was dealing with. In order to get close to me it was gone take people that I trusted because I never been the type to trust people.Ex Shreveport detective Rodney Demery was the illustrator to this plot Rodney Demery was Dexter Demery first cousin and Dexter was my ex wife old man he was locked up when I met her so she said but I later found out he was home when I met her.Rodney Demery was also close family to Shuntina them, the hoova boys are Shuntina them people is it starting to sink in to my readers yet.All this time had past so It was difficult for me to put it together at first but when the most high God YAHWEH wants something to be known no force on earth can stop it.Tavara

George and trigger played it so raw that it is unreal.They crossed me with my kids moms,family, friends and all,now the government applied pressure to them and put them in fear against me... Shirley gray was my ex wifeTamesha Grimas was my side line girl Tamesha was jet black shoulder length hair and super fine all though she was not the prettiest face to the eyes but her body in go getter status made up for what the face lacked . Shirley was a red bone that stood about 5"11 good hair that came to the middle of her shoulders with a body that was so thick and,ass shaped like a NBA ball she had two goals in her mouth.All she did was work are at least I thought not knowing she was the main player under me .She was working at lsu hospital when I met her we met each other at auto zone on Greenwood road never knowing she would be the one to cross me trying to collect inheritance.You see my Bloodline are the Dukes of nobility the Rockefeller Family and the Rothschild family with a account at Fidelity investments in biotechnology this account is over 24.6 TRILLION dollars as of January 2017.My DNA TYPE IS THE RAREST rhnull blood in the world scientists call it the GOLDEN BLOOD AND WILL PAY MIL-

LIONS FOR MY BLOOD TYPE.Problem is that it was only nine people in the world that have this blood type.When I was shot up from the government hit my blood had to be flown from overseas by the Netherlands one one in the the united States could give me blood.Rhnull the blood type I have all great leaders kings have that blood type it's a royalty blood type do your research on rhnull blood this is the blood type of Yashua JESUS Christ had.I will get into it more later in this chapter. Shatory was working with them I think the whole time but somewhere down the line she told me about this dude named Jamie Prince aka big woo are Shay she told me this when she was staying on Darien in QB.. Shatory was bout 5"9 fine as hell beautiful and a super super freak one who loved sucking dick and swallow all the cum and wake you up in the morning with it again.I was told that this dude Shay was hating on me so bad and was saying all type of shit about me Shatory asked me did I know him I replied no which I didn't at that time.Shay was Calvin Reed homie that I later found out from shay he told me not knowing he was telling me.Now at this time I still don't know about the GOVERNMENT plot but I knew something was not making since. Many people played a role in this GOVERNMENT murder plot upon my life even my Mother yes America my suppose to be mother Teretha MERRITT my sister's as well. I'm going to skip to the night I was shot I will list all names of those I know that took part in this plot at the end of this book.November 26 2010 I was at my son mother's house cooling with my son I get a call from Decoryon saying he want couple pounds my son begged me not to go that night I remember my son who was 6 at the time said daddy you don't have to go my mommy don't get off till 7am you can sleep in my bed with me.And we can play the game all night daddy please don't go never the less I went,reassuring my son Caleb that I would be back in 30 minutes. He looked at me, with a look in his eyes as if he felt something wrong and, it was his job to make his dad stay.I made it to my townhouse which was in Sherwood townhomes about 10 minutes from my son house.The crazy part about all this is I get a call from trigger one day telling me he sat outside my townhouse waiting for me to come out so he could murder me I immediately went to his mom house with my 40 caliber he came running out with a 357 only to get drew down on from me he jumped and hid behind a tree so out of me having love for his mommy I told him I would not kill him at his mommy house.At this time trig stayed across the street from my lil brother pig.I told trig I was going to his house and if he come to his own house I was gone murder him in broad open day light. Trig mommy house was only two minutes from his house by the time i got there trig had called my lil brother pig telling him I drew down on him.As I'm pulling up my lil brother come running out saying big bro trig just called and told me so i stopped his words saying if trig come to his house I'm going to murder him in his own yard my lil bro knew I meant what I said.I waited for two hours trig never came, But back to me at my townhouse to get the pounds to go meet deco- ryon I grab the two pounds he claim he wanted.I remember standing in my kitchen and hearing a voice saying don't go once again I failed to listen to the voice of protection YAHWEH.I walked out the door with the two pounds and got into the gray Monte Carlos 2004. I had set the deal up to meet at the Chevron gas station on the corner of HOLLYWOOD and Hearne Ave Decoryon called and changed the meet place saying he had a flat tire.I left the store to go two streets down to where he said he was.I get there I don't see the car so I call him no answer. My first mind said leave you don't need that 1300 dollars my second mind said call him again so I did still.I know many are wondering why did I leave the spot where I set up shop to meet him at only because he said he had a flat tire.But I call the second time no answer my heart tells me not to call a third time once again I don't listen to what my heart told me.I call a third time he picks up on the third ring.I asked what car was he in cause I didn't see the multiple color 80 model Chevy he told me man by bad I be getting these street confused because I'm not from over here. I asked what street he was on because he told me to come on Essex street he told me he was on Virginia which was the cross street.i asked was he walking he said yes he had to get a jack from his homie..At this time he turned the corner him and another guy decoryon has on all brown with thick brown gloves and the other guy martez loston has on all red but he keeps walking while decoryon stands on the corner looking to see what car I was in if I knew that they had this plan I could have killed him on the corner.He finally see me because I'm directing him to me which car he gets to the car.He get to the car and opened the passenger door the car interior light comes on when he opened the door and he pause.He gets in the car leave the passenger door ajar,we greet one another the pounds are on the passenger floor board he ask is that the pounds I state yes he picks them up because there were in a bag he opens a bag and say damn big man that smell good I tell that shit some flame he state 1300 I say yes he said I got 1275 big man I'm like fuck it come on with it.He goes to go in his pocket my mind said everything straight business Rico where the other nigga he was with at.I take my eyes off decoryon to look to see where martez went as soon, as my eyes made contact with my driver side window decoryon opens fire on me the first three shot hitting me in the chest before i realized what was happening. I said fuck, robbery, and hit the gas to the floor I sped off.I remember feeling two are three more shots.one shot in the finger and one to the back of the shoulder which that shot ran me in the right side ditch.A s I hit the ditch my feet is still on the pedal and one hand on the wheel my car is still pulling trying to get out the ditch. I remember thinking to myself if I don't come out this ditch these niggas gone kill me out here God YAHWEH pushed it out the mud and dirt back on solid gravel.The tires touched the pavement and left marks all the way to the corner upon coming out the ditch I was shot in the right side of the chest I turn the corner and speed three four streets down to Tamesha Grimas house.A s I'm speeding to her house I scream fuck I let these lil niggas kill me I remember hearing a deep voice say son you are not bleeding from the mouth you OK.Right after, this same voice said my child don't panic. and said in a more commanding voice slow your breathing for you are okay my breathing slowed and heart stopped racing upon hearing this voice command.I pull in Mesha yard blowing the horn as if I had laid on it until she came out it was 19 degrees on this night in 2010.Mesha came out and went back in I laid on the horn again this time she came out she had a coat on by that time I was almost to the stairs of her porch.She said Cortez what you blowing that horn like that for crazy.At that time I was standing in the porch light about to walk up the steps that's when she sees me bloody from my shirt down to my polo boots.She scream and cries and run in the house to grab the phone. I make my enter into the front door of the house by this time she made it back to the front door she stops me, and push me back out the door.I tell her to get the pounds out of the car before the laws get there.The only way I knew the pounds was still in the car on the floor was when I pulled up in the yard...I didn't realize I didn't put the car in park and it began to roll and with the driver side door open the interior light was on allowed me to see the pounds as I put the car in park.Mesha has got the pounds out the car and on the phone with 911 they asking her where was I hit at she replies.SHE DONT know I'm bloody from my shirt to my shoes they tell her to raise my shirt to see where I'm hit and she does and cries harder seeing six holes five in my chest one in my stomach.ROD-NEY DEMERY was there before the fire truck the ambulance are any police.i said two prayers that night one to stay and one if I had died..When I said those prayers it was a peace I never felt in life I was not worried about anything despite the situation.The ambulance got there and rushed me to the hospital.T he paramedics counted 23 total gunshot wounds i got to Lsu and was rushed directly to surgery.I was stuck in the neck with sedation and 3 seconds after it was lights out.......

THE FACTS AND EVIDENCE

Over time, facts and evidence with, Federal documents and Audio recordings and the guilty heart of some of those that took part.C ould only tell me in ways that showed they feared for there life from the government that applied pressure to those around me...........I awake from a six hour surgery to find myself in great pain. The doctor assigned to watch over me until I woke up came rushing over to me the first thing he said is do you know where you at ,then he said right after that ,was you are on life support and, have a tube in your mouth so u can't talk and ,asked did I understand that and told me blink once for yes twice for no.I blinked once,then he asked me again do I know where I'm at I blinked once again, then he asked did I remember what happened for me to be there. I blinked once again.He asked did I remember having surgery I didn't blink at all he smiled cause he knew I was fully alert at this time. Now he begins to tell me,all that is wrong and what was done he started off with the surgery telling me I had to have surgery on my diaphragm because, one of the bullets put a whole in it said it took two stitches to close and ,22 staples to close my stomach up. Then he moved the gown so I could see my eyes was wide open upon seeing it. Then he said you are on life support because your right lung collapsed and it was a inflatable balloon to lift my lung up and I'm not breathing on my own ,and told me to look to your right at the life support machine. I did and seen the machine breathing for me , my eyes watered up with raged. The heart machine started beeping real fast so the doctor knew why ,and told me to calm myself down.After, he was sure, I was calm he went on to tell me about the rest, telling me I have a chest tube because the five holes in my chest THAT caused blood to back up in my chest and said the chest machine sucks that blood out my chest.He stated to me that I was hit nine times ,with 23 total gunshot holes and told me everywhere I was shot .5 times in the chest,once in the left leg,twice in the right lung,twice in the back of the shoulder once in the left hand,twice in the right hand and, once in the stomach.He told me my hands was wrapped up because ,all my bones were shattered, in both my hands and, I may not be able to use some of my fingers.Then, he told me I have two waiting rooms ,full of people to see me and he smiled and asked did I want them to come in. I blinked once he said it's to many so we are only going to let your immediate family in to see you everyone else can't I blinked once.At this time, I'm going back in because, the effects of the medicine is still active I see so many come in but I'm drifting I hear everyone saying different things but I feel people holding my thumbs and I hear prayers I open my eyes I see TAMESHA,SHIRLEY,MY MOMMY,MY LIL SISTER CANDY,MY COUSIN ROBERT EARL,MY BRO TONY,MY LIL BRO PIG GOING OFF,I SEE MY NIECE,RODNEY DE-MERY,SHUNDA HOLMES AND MANY MANY OTHER PEOPLE.Rodney Demery and Shunda HOLMES are the detectives Demery and my lil bro pig not seeing eye to eye because pig going crazy and Demery telling him to come down.But, pig wasn't hearing nothing until my mommy Teretha MERRITT calmed him down.Im faded again I hear this voice say, uncle fight ,my uncle a survivor he gone pull through he already in survival mode it was my niece.Her voice I heard over all others for some reason Demery was all in my face asking questions seeing I'm on life support and can't talk he still asking questions.I'm just looking at him as if he had to be slow, time would soon show, he was what I thought..Not knowing that many that was at the hospital that night ,knew why i was there and time would soon reveal it with, undeniable facts and evidence.Tavara was at the hospital everyday acting as if she truly cared knowing, the role she and many others played in it .The next day are so ,I was moved off the critical floor to my room where the flood of people came everyday.At least for one day.. Because I'm in my room on the first day and the room phone rings, and my twins mother picks it up and answer it she passes it to me. I ask who it was she said someone named d saying he my cousin his daddy name Johnny ray Dukes.I have no one kin to me by that name, that I'm aware of.I get the phone and say who this he tell me d and tell me the same thing he tells my twins mother Gladys Smith.He tells me, that he heard what happened and wanted to see me and asked what room I'm in it must was a look on my face that was uneasy ,cause my twins mother knew I didn't know who this was.I was in room k-8 on the eighth floor I told d I was on the 3rd floor in room 219.When I passed the phone back to Gladys to hang up ,she was looking at me with that look like she knew something but I just didn't know what.She hangs the phone up and ,say you don't know who that was do you I told her no. My mommy was in the room and a couple more other people so they look at each other and ,my mother called the head doctor in. They said something to each other about 30 mins later the doctor comes back with a arm band.I have a arm band on all ready so, I'm wondering what that is for so he tells me what is going on.He tells me ,that the arm band is my new name John Doe and said my name want be listed if you call the hospital because they don't want them to come finish the job. So my family told them to do so and security is on high alert.Shirley was my girlfriend at the time at least the main one when she came in the room it was like she was pissed are afraid are envy to see me still alive.She sat in the chair away from me while Gladys sat on the other side on the couch I asked Shirley, why she was sitting so far then she pulled the chair closer I asked her what was wrong and where was she when I was in surgery because she wasn't at work cause she worked at LSU. The hospital I was rushed to,I looked at her and said I was told you had something do with this her eyes went to darting across the room non stop she messing with her fingers.Im knowing that look on her face it's the look damn he know I'm lying but then she replied i ain't did shit I don't know what happened to you. OOOOOOO BUT TIME WOULD SOON TELL AND PROVE THE OPPO-SITE.AT THIS time Gladys gets mad and say she was bout to go I told her she didn't have to be-cause I wanted her to stay.She had been there and had her stuff brought to her to stay with me for more days.Gladys only went to work other then that she was at the hospital with me.So she get her things and leave before she passes the bed,she looks at Shirley with a look of disgust as if she KNEW FOR A FACT SHIRLEY WAS LY-ING.Gladys gets to the door and, Demery met her because he was bout to come in but he sees Gladys coming out so he steps out with her.I always have asked her what Demery and her was talking about.Demery comes in, now Shirley says she has to get back to work and Shunda HOLMES is stand-ing to the side now it's time for them to talk to me. Demery starts off by, introducing himself and

HOLMES he then ask me what happened before I could reply. HOLMES tell me not to trust my brother greedy and told me your COUSIN Tavara ain't your people don't trust her either.Then ,Demery started his questions Demery asks what happened I tell him it was a robbery he asked was it planned was I pose to be dropping something off. I said no.He said to me how did this happen. I said I had just dropped my homie off and ,was pulling of when a guy walking down the street at that time shunda HOLMES tells me to stop .Because she needs to get this on recorder.She grabs a recorder because she has two of them she sit one on the table in front of me and,push play.I start over I said as I did at first it was a guy walking that asked if I had a light I said yes as I reached in my pocket to give him a light when I looked up he was telling me to give it up. Demery asked what made the guy pull his gun, and who was the homeboy I had dropped off. I said my money slid out my pocket when I pulled the lighter out HOLMES asked was it a wad of money? I replied i wouldn't call 600 700 dollars a wad it was bill money but I guess to him it was a wad she say continue.I said so when I see the gun next thing I know the guy began shooting and I smashed out.Demery laughed a little and looked at me and said do you know you died last night .I said no because no one told me that he stated yes your heart stopped for about 2 minutes and started back beating on its on.Then he says you gone sit right there and not gone tell us what happened and ,said we didn't find no guns are drugs so you not the suspect, you are the victim.I looked at him eye to eye and told him do he think if I knew who shot me I wouldn't tell him? I said the same thing he said I died that night at that time he told me.That they found two different shell cases in my car 380 caliber shell cases, on the driver side floor and 9 mm on the driver side floor and asked did I have a gun. I laughed and said you just told me you didn't find any guns but to answer your question no.I did not at that time the questions stop.Now HOLMES has something to say she pulls the second recorder out and says all this time you dealing all these pounds throughout the city and you was completely under all our radar.She said when we got to the hospital it was two waiting rooms full of people for you she said it was so many that many had to leave the waiting area and wait somewhere else because other people family are there to see them to.Then she said she said to herself, either this guy a celebrity ,are he very loved and very very popular.Until, they got a hold to my brother greedy then she pressed play on the second recorder and his voice comes on he tells them that.I was the pound man I was fucking with the Cartel I buy pounds for 450 and sold them for 600 are 650 that I supplied a piece of the Cooper Road, Mooretown , Cedar Grove, Ingleside queensbourgh and a part of HOLLYWOOD and he mentioned a guy named K who he said was my main supplier. After she cut it off I told them if my brother told y'all that then they need to go pick him back up because he knows more bout my life then I do.They looked at each other and left and said there interview me was down and they would contact me if they needed any further information.Now while I'm in the hospital the drawing blood seem like very damn hour, they told me that I had a fever that they was trying to figure out why it wouldn't break so they realized that my blood was to low and I lost to much blood from being shot and having the major surgery I had to have a blood transfusion they found a donor overseas and told me I got that golden blood at that time I had no clue of what GOLDEN BLOOD WAS.They said it was gone take 48 hours for my blood to arrive the head surgeon walked in and told me I'm blessed and whatever calling GOD HAS PLACED ON ME HE SUGGEST I DO IT CAUSE I HAVE TRULY A GREAT PURPOSE ON EARTH.Then he pulled the x-ray chart out and clicked on the light on the x ray board.He placed the chart on the board then looked at me and said do you see this clear line going toward the shaded section.He said the shaded area is your heart and the light area with the line is the path the bullet going then he said if he said it was a medical explanation for what he was about to say he would be lying in his 26 years of being a surgeon he never have seen this.He pointed at the light line and said there was not any bone are anything that would make the bullet deflect and go the other way.He stated it was nothing but flesh the bullet was a half of hair from my heart and made a U-turn and it was not in my chest.They did ex ray after ex ray on my chest no trace of that bullet his eyes started to water up and he told me son this is truly a act of God and there is no medical explanation for that and told me to find my calling cause you have a great purpose to do he wiped his eyes and walked out.. December 6 2010 I was discharged.I went home with a lot on my mind ..First thing was the shooters I knew it was two which is why decoryon opened fire because he thought I seen martez walking up on my car.This explain the 380 shell cases on the driver side floor board that Demery mentioned at the hospital this also explain how Demery told my family it was a hit before he ever talked to me. Next thing was, to find out who this colorful box Chevy belong to and find out what the fuck is going on.I hollered at a couple people about the box Chevy and within three weeks BOOSIE told me who it was his mommy and who they run with.I did some more research and find out martez was my baby mother Thressa Brown cousin Thressa was a x Caddo Correctional officer and a caddo sheriff until her heart problem.I have a baby for Sherika SANDERS, Don Otis daughter, retired,caddo sheriff and, Shreveport police..I make it to my townhouse and notice a blue unmarked impala sitting right in the view of my townhouse.I go In and have a seat I still got pounds to sell I holla at one of my niggas and we get them gone.I stay home bout a day are two and I understand I can't do shit for myself so I call my bby and tell her i need to lay low because I'm to hurt she told me baby come

on i got you and you know I do and my other little lady Anita Williams.Who nursed me when I
wasn't at the other house however the first was my
bby.Naquita Burton was my baby.I m at quita
house for sometime healing and cooling with bae
and thinking about everything piece by piece.It
took time for me to hold tissue to whip my ass tissue felt like it weighed 100 pounds I cried cause I
couldn't do the most simple thing like whipping
my own ass..A person don't truly understand the
most simple thing until one finds himself are herself not able to do it not because they don't want
to but because they cant that is one of the most
hurting feelings in the world.At this time I'm just
doing my research on everything but I still have
no clue this was a government hit.It would be a
few years before I would find out.Much time past
and I gained much evidence about the entire plot
upon me and from who what and why.My journey in finding out that so many people family
friends kids mother's knew of this plot upon me
wouldn't truly begin until I found what my true
calling was to be the voice of the people this began
within my civil rights movement the truth would
reveal.That would show the world beyond a reasonable doubt that the most high GOD YAHWEH

MEANT FOR THE WORLD TO SEE AND
KNOW.

THE CIVIL RIGHTS MOVEMENT

Pressure

No.Now, the Civil Rights movement is why The MOST HIGH GOD YAHWEH SPARED my LIFE. You see he needed my full attention and time, for the journey that was plan since August 26 1979 since the birth of a King and leader.One must be awakened from a sleep before one can lead The people of a nation.....After five are, six years after I was shot up, I find out many things from close people. But I was still without the major pieces that would make all this make since at this point I'm getting frustrated about many things and the Most High knew his son was.So many people that took part in this that, wanted me to think I was going crazy only because, they knew there role within this plot.And feared for the world to know and see the truth of who they truly are.As I stated in the earlier chapter of what Sheria foster asked me about had I did something to the government.My twins mother Gladys Smith told me about Things started to changed right before George came home and told me George and Tavara was the ones telling all those lies.One night George called me and told me something of very great importance.T his was right after sponky loc robbed him in our cousin Shunda Dukes yard. This was right after he told me bout him and our cousin having a fight.My little cousin GC GEORGE CALVIN LEE called me and said Rico they want me to murder you.He said Rico I told them we wasn't raised to kill our family then he said I love you big cuz I love you they gone have to do what they got to do.We wasn't raised to kill our family me and Gc cried on the phone that night I told him to pray and asked Gc who is they, he never told me who they was however I already knew who they was they government which Rodney Demery applied the pressure.Gc told me that Shunda Dukes set him up in her yard for sponky loc to rob him I asked him how did it happen.He said Rico Shunda called me to bring her something and when I got there sponky loc r him and I asked him, did Shunda ever come outside he said no.So he goes back to saying Rico I love you big cuz no matter what we been through,no matter what I love you big cuz.This was in 2016 close to the end of the year.I called and aware Shreveport internal affairs Greg Jackson of what was going on and told him that my cousin life was in danger for not killing me the entire Shreveport police department knew of this.One day later I get a call from the Louisiana Attorney general office from a Shreveport u.s. Marshall about the GOVERN-MENT murder hit upon me.He tells me that they see and hear everything I have been exposing and they want me to keep applying pressure to the feds cause they don't know why the feds have not filed charges on any of this.He asked had I ever did any kind of work for the government to have the account I own and asked have I ever had a important case with the government I told him no. Then I asked why did he ask that he replied because he trying to see if it was something I had on the government to why are how I own this account but stated once again we see everything that is going on and we see you are not lying.He told me that I'm gone have to go sit down with a federal agent in person so the case can be charged and, said the United States Marshall can only arrest someone when the feds put the call to them.I told him the hit come from the federal government before I could get my words out my mouth he said I see what is going on the feds tied in it.I told him he was a smart man he laughed and said it was his job.He asked was I mad enough to go to war with the government for what the GOVERNMENT has did to me I tell him no but however I will not stop applying pressure about it he stated that's what the Louisiana Attorney general wants me to do and said this was the reason for his call to me.In 2016 I move to Dallas TX in order to figure out more.Remember the blue round body Chevy I mentioned in the earlier chapter the GOVERNMENT plot.This Chevy belonged to this guy drew from the Cooper Road his baby mother used to do my hair at one time.Now my brother greedy stayed across the street from her.When i was still in Shreveport I'm talking to my brother and this same Chevy pulls in the church next door to my brother house.He see the Chevy I grab my gun because at this time I'm aware of the government murder plot but still have no clue that this is the Chevy that Tavara told me about came on Milton Street looking for me.I wouldn't find that out until

I moved to Texas.Back to my brother see the Chevy he holler and say that my boy drew he stay in Texas he gets out the car and go sit in the car for a few minutes with drew then he comes back and get in the car with me.He looks at me and out the blue he says lil brother slow down, I asked him what was he talking about he only said,I'm just saying slow down.I told him you didn't just say that for nothing, you said it for a reason i told him that before that car pulled up, and you went got in the car with him we was laughing and talking but, after you get out the car with him your whole mood different. I asked him again what he meant by that and why did he say that he got quite.I just looked at him he couldn't look me in my eyes... Tavara is the plot information source my cousin Nikki was Tavara second victim Tavara gave our cousin Nikki the pill that killed her the police went picked Tavara up about it and kept her for hours about it.She cried like a baby, my Aunt Ruth is who applied pressure about it. Now, how are why she wasn't charged I never understood it then but, I do now because she was apart of something much more bigger. One night on July 4 I'm not exactly sure of the exact year but it was between

2002 and 2006 I send Tavara to Subway on Kings highway across the street from university hospital to get me something to eat.She goes and get it and comes back I had not ate anything that day but what see brought back to me.I ate the food it was about 9 10 that night.At about 12 that night I get a pain within my stomach at first it felt that I had to shit very bad but, upon doing so it intensified the pain and got worse I thew up so many times until I was throwing up the yellow acid that breaks your food down.At bout 2am that morning the pain was unbearable and I told my cousin to rush me to the hospital.Upon arriving at Lsu I immediately was sent to the back they hooked me up to IVs and began to draw blood take blood pressure the final conclusion from doctors medical reports I was poisoned but my body had push 86 percent of the poison out by the time i arrived but they was for sure I was poisoned but, couldn't detect it because my body was rejecting it they was for certain and wrote it in the medical findings.Lakreshia Smith was at the hospital with me that night when the blood work came back she says to me o yea this what I wanted to here and the doctor read the paperwork negative of HIV and all other tests and he stated the findings of why I was there for poison

Gastro indigestion..The doctor asked did I eat anything that night I told him yes subway that my cousin brought to me about two are three hours before my arrival.He asked me did I eat anything else that day I told him no.Weeks later I went to lawyer Rodney Piper to open up a lawsuit upon subway with my medical records to show the cause.Never knowing I should have been opening a Criminal investigation upon my on family. I will get back to me moving to Texas in a minute before I left Shreveport god sent me a message through a chosen messenger.Ms C called my little sister candy and told her to have me call her are for my sister to bring me to her. She said God told her to deliver a very important message to me directly now this is someone I know but have not seen the sweet old lady in over 20 years.I tell my sister to come and pick me up and take me to her. Around this time god had already showed me the evil and satanic powers that lurked around me and I didn't know why but on this day I would find out why. Me and my sister and my nephew my sister son pull into the yard of Ms C house I get out the car and Ms C stands up, and walk off her porch into her yard she gives me a hug and tears roll down her cheeks.Im looking into her eyes I see those years are true genuine tears from her heart.She tells me Rico GOD has put me on her heart heavy and Everytime he do she cries and it's river of tears.She said she asked GOD why do she cry so strong when he place me on her heart she said God told her that the tears she cry are tears of joy.She said Rico GOD TOLD ME TO TELL YOU that you are not crazy he had to take you through what you went through because where he bout to take you to.She said GOD told me to tell you it's many evil spirits that wish to destroy you.She told me God told me to tell you that the reason these spirits want me destroyed is because I have a gift that is so strong and so power the world want be able to denie.Its as if she read my mind I was about to ask and she said no I don't know your gift GOD told me to tell you that he will reveal it to you when you ready.I look at her tears are flowing down her face at this point she tells my GOD said don't worry about all the houses cars money and people the enemy made you lose GOD TOLD ME TO TELL YOU HE ABOUT TO BLESS YOU ABUNDANTLY.SHE TOLD GOD SAID YOUR GIFT WILL MAKE YOUR ENEMIES TERRIBLE WITH FEAR then she went on to tell me about the angel of death curse that was released over me.I told her god had already showed me that she said God told me to tell you he GOT YOU. She put holy oil upon my head and prayed then she prayed in a language I didn't understand but,I felt the power of it to my soul and tears ran down my FACE not having a clue what she was saying but, my spirit did.We talked bout many other things after awhile me and my sister left to go back to our house but I would have a lot on my heart and mind that message was my confirmation of everything I had seen and learned was true and those that wanted me to think I was crazy would soon show I had great sense. But, this would be the start of a long journey that would lead to many many people being involved.This murder plot starts with my home city Shreveport Louisiana and goes to Dallas Texas, Arlington TX, California,Plano Texas... Now let's get back to me moving to Texas this is where my civil rights movement would start.This is where all proof would come out all that took part and all.This where all the recordings would come.I move to Texas to get away and to think and put this together I move with my niece I stayed a couple nights at my mom's house, me and my oldest bro had words I still don't know what this was about but we quashed it. So I'm at my niece house in Dallas I had already got a job at ups while at my mom's house for the couple days I was there.The area where my niece stayed was a cool little area the scene was a new one.I would soon feel it out and the people around it and what it knew and had to offer.I start working at ups making 11.00 dollars working part time it was a cool lil job but not when you have child support payments COMING out a 18 to 20 hours a week job 70 80 sometimes 100 a week it got so bad I went to see my parole officer in Louisiana he seen my check and told me it don't do me no good to go..But, never the less I hung in there for six months and did my thing on the side I had started to feel my way around.But I'm still in a tight spot all though I did have a female name LAtrica now LAtrica stood about six feet big titties sexy and beautiful.She rocked with me for a minute.i had already started to learn what I was chosen to do and was teaching here about what happened and why and I was getting into learning the law at this time.I remember many nights me her and my niece used to sit in smoke and I tell them how big my journey is and how great God has chosen me to be and the many things that will come.I used to sit at my niece house at the table and write read and study till sometimes day light and then some more.I started off learning about the illegal banking Cartel the Federal reserve the IRS and the treasure department and depository trust and clearing. That portion would lead me to the major source surrounding my situation all those entities surround the foundation of the government murder plot.The FEDERAL reserve controls the entire united States with the illegal Federal reserve note dollars the FEDERAL reserve is a foreign corporation stated by CFR 1-895-1 income devired from a central foreign banking institution that the Constitution states is ILLEGAL as well. This led me to the birth certificate and that would be the key to unlock this GOVERNMENT murder plot and why so many feared to speak.T he bar code on each birth certificate makes each birth certificate a negotiable instrument meaning it can be sold traded for profit.Each birth certificate is tied to the FEDERAL reserve depository trust and clearing and the treasure department and wall Street yes wall Street they control it all.Private foreign billion Aires controlling your every dollar thought and moves .My birth certificate is tied to a 24.6 trillion dollar account at Fidelity investments that is held at the Chicago Federal reserve Bank.T his account is in biotechnology all pharmacy drugs and military chemical weapons.The military needs this account to run its illegal military operations.The plot was to turn people against me so I would have no one to go to are turn to by creating lies that they knew are easily moved on the brain of the weak.See with a person having no one are no where to run to are with out money to move around makes it very hard to achieve things.Only YAHWEH the Most High god can protect you in this time.Dealing with this you face the powers that be and those that the power that be have paid off.By finding this out about the Federal reserve led me to find my account that made since to what many people had told me.I remember being at different places and people that knew me knew about this account and I didn't used to say.Rico I hear you rich I used to think at that time they was speaking about me selling pounds I would reply I'm not rich I sell a few pounds but Im no where near rich.T hey would reply no nigga I heard you got millions but acting like you don't got it the look that they would have in there eyes told me they were so very serious. On this one day not

long after I was released from doing my 5 year
sentence which I had to serve 2 years of it. I went
to one of my ex houses lamora Bryant as soon as I
walked in she sat straight up and said damn you
look like money. Her brother meechie was real
close to decoryon Reed when I met lamora her lil
bro was in jail this was in 2007 she had told me she
told her bro about I was the pound man. I would
never meet meechie until 2013 at Shreveport
Louisiana work release while serving my two
years from the 5 year sentence I found out because he told me what she had told him. At this
time I'm still not knowing he was close to decoryon but lamora and meechie both knew from
day one.All this made since with my account ,the
millions many people knew of my wealth but failing to inform me of it.The plot that is upon me
was, a well thought out process of, deception, lies
and crosses, that took many years to put in play
.By, many close people that feared the government and killers that worked for them.W hile in
Texas as I said the Federal reserve led me to my
biotechnology account see, a promissory note is a
form of legal tender. Let me take a little time to
explain this to you each and every American birth
certificate comes with a bar code first all one must

understand what can be bar coded. Only PRO-
DUCE AND PRODUCT CAN BE BAR. CODED
for sale, trade, are profit Human being are not pro-
duce nor product. When a child is born the hospital creates a LIVE CERTIFICATE OF BIRTH the
hospital sends it to the Treasure department and
the treasure department sends it to depository
trust and clearing they enter it into the book keeping data base as merely a piece of paper.birth depository trust and clearing send the live certificate
of birth back as a birth certificate making you a
negotiable instrument..I know many may say
what's the difference a live certificate of birth tells
that you are a live 1 you and your parents it will
not be with a bar code because it proves you living
human being boy are girl it tells your medical status of you and your parents.The birth certificate
only tell if you are black are white boy are girl and
your parents place of address and where you were
born. A dog has a birth certificate that states the
dog name weather it's a boy are girl the dog address the dog parents and both the human birth
certificate and a animal birth certificate comes
with a bar code.You can do your own research
and find out more are follow the documents I
have expose d to the world.Without me learning

about the Federal reserve it would have been near difficult to trace the account to Fidelity investments and the Chicago Federal reserve Bank.. Texas was where I started the civil rights movement at in the beginning that would be the start of the truth unfolding about the GOVERNMENT murder hit.Living in Texas I started to meet different forms of people that was having there own Radio shows political people.The first Radio show I did exposing the United States government was on ktox 1340am on Luca Zanna love guns and freedom radio.This was the night before Carrollton Texas police killed my nephew at the motel 6 Malcolm Hickson .I spoke about many things on love guns and freedom radio that night the next morning which is when they killed my nephew they waited for him to come out the motel room and a sniper shot him in the chest.The next few days go by and the cia reach out to me saying they think it was a political killing for the recordings I got against the GOVERNMENT. The motel where he was killed at the police say it was not one working camera and they claim none of the officers Had on a body cam.A t this time I was fucking with this lady name Chrystal WYNCH I'm not sure if she was working with the people the whole time but I'm for certain she played her role within Texas after I moved to Texas the government hit followed me not knowing it was already there. Chrystal was a older female with two kids on was a Denton county probation officer and now she's a Dallas probation officer.You see Chrystal had her daughter run everything about me and had her daughter contact Rodney Demery not Knowing I was on top of everything by that time.I n order to catch a snake one must not fear a snake .Chrystal was the type that thought she was slick but wasn't slick enough sometimes trying to be to slick are just slick at all can put you and your game at risk of being seen.Texas brought many different things to the table regarding the murder plot at this time I'm gaining access to many platforms and not once did my mom ever tell me she was proud I understand why now she knew she was the key that held a very major part.

INJUSTICE IN AMERICA

Freedom from injustice

This is the injustice we are faced with throughout America the government installs fear within the people to be afraid of what they know is right and true.Now my mother knew of this plot since the beginning I remember my sister Nikki and I got into it when I was like 17 are 18 I remember her saying with your hiv having ass.Right after that I get a call from my mommy telling me Nikki didn't mean that and she was just mad I paid my sister no mind anyway. Not knowing that my own family was the biggest part of this GOVERN-MENT murder plot.You see my mom went to school are something with Shuntina goines mommy are, aunt my sister Nikki, used to talk to Hoova James.One day I was like 18 and was at one of my female friends house named Lashunda

Hardy, and Hoova James was her people. I think but, anyway he starts talking to me saying, his people wanted him to be apart of some very satanic shit, and he said, you ain't did nothing to me.I said me what the fuck you mean I ain't, he then tried to clean it up saying I'm not talking bout you Im just saying but, the look he had in his eyes told me a lot more then his mouth.He went on to say, that he told his people that he wasn't gone take any part in it he told me they cut his dope supply off for not doing so.Hoova James, was Shuntina goines family, he was a close family member to them this what Hoova James told me, would be very important information later on in LIFE. Remember when I said in the last chapter that not once, did my mother ever tell me she was proud of me let fill you in.My mom knew, I was very close to finding this murder plot out and, knew that it would lead back to her knowing of it from the start. So I could understand why I never heard those words I'm proud of you.Why would one be proud of someone who suppose to be dead BUT, he's getting closer to finding the truth out about you.While I'm with Chrystal I guess my mom and Chrystal didn't know I knew they was communicating on a very different levels certain things Chrystal would say only one person could know.My niece, told me one day that I was gone run across something that would make the government want to murder me. Something that I don't suppose to know but, I would soon find out what she meant.One day Chrystal and I was at the store, where I used to be at and her play nephew pulls up.Now I remember her saying she been waiting on him to show up and, she just kept saying this over days as if she wanted me to hear it. On this night, he finally does, and she gets out and go sit in the car with him then, she rolls the passenger side window down,and tells me he said what's up.I speak to him and ask if he got some green with him he tells me yes.I tell him what I got then Chrystal say baby show him what you working with I said huh she says the iron I said o I didn't know what you was talking about.So I hold it up just enough for him to see a piece of it.I read his lips and, Chrystal lips he says I can pop him right now. He must had already had his hand on his gun cause I seen Chrystal put her hand on his hand and hear her tell him nawl not now just be cool.So he tells me it's nice what I had and showed me his and then asked how long would it take me to get off of a pack.Now mind you I never asked for a pack this was part of the plot and play that Chrystal felt I never knew of.I tell him a time frame, him and her chop it up for a few more minutes then she gets out and comes back in get in the car,and pass me the pack.I look at her, in tell her i just heard what you told him and read his lips, she denied it, but I wasn't asking I was telling her.Her plan was to try in use her nephew to do the job and to get me jammed up, so the beef would start to try in carry the plot out. She watched every move I made, and I watched every thought she made keeping me ahead of the snake at all times.A few days pass I had already dumped almost all of it.I leave the store on this night and go to her house where she was and still lives with her sister. I get there I sit outside in the car and blew a blunt .This is on December 23 2017 I go to the back of the house put most of what I had in the back yard and keep a little with me and I get back in the car.She calls in ask what I was doing I told her I just got done smoking and was bout go to the store and grab some Newport's and cigars.I leave and get to the store which was about 3 min-utes from her house I get there no cars at all are in the parking lot I go in buy what I came for upon walking out the 7)11 store I see a Dallas lady police officer but I'm in Carrollton.She looks and she me and immediately turn around and speed walk back to her truck at this time I still have not made it to the car once I get to the car I back up and make it to the street i turn on to the street and look in my review mirror I see the Carrollton police truck but the lady police officer is a Dallas police in Carrollton.I see the truck turn behind me I continue to drive I finally get to mayflower street where I had just left as soon as I turn on Mayflower Street the law turns behind me as well. The police truck still has not pulled me over yet.I pull in front of the house and, cut the car off and open the door, the police hit the lights.Everyrhing that was done was illegal on top of that, Chrystal is the one that put them on me.They search the car and find under a half ounce of weed Chrystal finally comes out the house as if she didn't know what was going on already knowing she the one who did it.Upon going to jail the police see my paperwork saying I'm a United States councilman and tells me they received a call from a lady telling them drugs was in the car. When the laws got to the car they kept asking where is the gun I just looked at them and said nothing it was no gun in the car however Chrystal thought it was one.

See Chrystal thought it would be a gun in the car with me and the green would be in there as well knowing that I had just smoked knowing that would make the laws do a illegal search her main pray was she was hoping a gun would be in the car so I could be charged with a felony and a misdemeanor and be in debt with her play nephew that could put the plot in motion on a reasonable cause owing money.Her plan didn't turn out how she had thought but her knowing she was my only co signer and knowing she was going out of town on the 23 of December which was the early morning I got arrested at about 2 r 3 am that night she was leaving at six AM knowing I would have to sit in there for three days till she got back.And knowing when she got back I would have to use some of the money to bond out with putting me in a deeper hole of paying the debt. February 10 2018 was another episode only this time cocaine was found when it was only weed that I had I was in jail for over 14 hours booked on weed and evading arrest 14 hours later I had a cocaine charged even the judge that set the back said that didn't sound right.Once again I was in Chrystal car and she knew I was on the way to her house it was police on almost every corner as if they was waiting to see that car..On this night of February 10 2018 after they arrest me and I'm sitting in the back of the police truck the officer that was on the passenger side ask if I was sick I asked him what the fuck hr mean and stated no and asked if he was sick.He replies I'm just asking a question and said he just doing his job I told him that isn't apart of his job if there is no injuries to the officer so I told him those questions that are asked at the jail.Chyrstal was playing her part well with the help of her daughter as the Dallas probation officer at this time I fully aware of the government plot and why but was still finding out all those that took are taken part.I bond out and I'm back at the store now things starting to reveal those that know of this plot That are the store. Now that I'm backing up from Chrystal I'm living at the budget suites me and Cortez Frazier aka iron head.Now, iron head was this type of person,he was in a car wreck and he crashed into the 18 Wheeler and the trailer of the truck fell on the car trapping iron head legs between the Trailer and crushed car. I met iron head like a year in half before and he was a cool lil dude but at the same time sneaky and loud that love to buy pussy and Gamble he didn't smoke weed but had many other habits. Like syrup, zannex bars, x pills, hydro pills. He had got a lil money back from the wreck bout a year before I met him.Any and every woman that came into the store he tells them they ain't got to pay for nothing and give them 70 80 dollars many people at the store seen his weakness and they soon sent his weakness to him knowing he loved to get fuck up to the max.Im living there for bout two days I had just bout a infinity j30 and went to Lancaster that night to go out to eat. When I left the store iron head was with his people he say.Let me stop hear and tell you about this female I met named NICOLE but I called her black, she was jet black,about five feet 6 inches and brick house fine. Big black pretty legs, big breast, and alot of ass and, a pussy that look like three camel toes.I met her on a dating site I talked to her for a few days and then we met each other in person after a few days..She came to the room I had and she was asking way to many questions that shouldn't have been asked on a first time of meeting someone.Me being me you can't catch a snake if you fear one I tell her you ask to many questions like you trying to find out information for someone.She replies but not just right off but she do reply with I just ask a lot of questions I tell her the question you ask are not questions of any first night answers. At this point I knew I need to keep her close to find out what I wanted to know one of her mane things was always wanting to know where I lived and who I deal with as in street wise. When I tell you she asked questions that would make ray Charles see I knew then either they have sent a damn fool to gain information are she just nosey as hell but I was leaning towards the first.Over time she she made many slip ups about things only someone that deals with the people that's against me would say.Everytime she would I would tell her just to see the reply she would give and Everytime her reply would let me know that the first thought I had was right..To give you a clear picture of a few of the things she would say are ask.One time she ask me about my ABA membership but claim she wanted to help with the fee but not ever once have she are did she.Another I asked why do she follow me on each and everything im on but she have no one she follow are that are following her.Many might say she could have just wanted to see what you got going on and I would say true but I would also tell you that I know who I'm up against and the way they MOVE

INFORMATION IS THE KEY THEY NEED. THROUGH out my journey of being on this movement I follow YAHWEH AND I HAVE NEVER BEEN MISLEAD AND HE SURE WOULD NOT START NOW ARE EVER.One night me and her was talking about some people that she knew played a very small role but yet they still played a role.Before I go on to tell you this I got to tell you that two of the people we was talking about that night one of those people she was going buying weed from but claim she didn't think it would matter if I knew are if I didn't know at this point in time I didn't know that they was playing a role but that still don't excuse that fact she was dealing with people she met only cause she knew me.But, I had no knowledge of them dealing with each other, the dude told me what was going on she got pissed with him asking why did he tell me. Remember I said to catch a snake you CANT FEAR ONE Back to the issue at hand when me and her was talking one night I'm telling her that when all this unfold that It would be alot of people involved, it was more people that I was talking about but it was only two people she was worried about and she told me this when I asked her.I told her out of all those names I said you only worried about two of them her reply was i ain't worried about no one else I asked her why she didn't get mad about Chrystal name her reply was I'm not worried about that bitch I asked why was she worried about Daryl and PISTOL she replied cause you lying on them.She knew the role they played cause we was living together at that time Remember when I said to catch a snake you can't be afraid of one now it's very clear who she was trying to gain information for. See sometimes all you have to do is have heart to face the enemy and they will tell you everything you need to know.I will give you one more clear picture one night we was talking and I asked her what was important to her she got mad and asked why I'm asking her that then told me I'm only asking her that only because what happened the night before I ask her what happened the night before she got quite and said she was answering nothing..She claim she rock with me AMERICA THEY DIDN'T TELL HER WHO I WAS THEY SHOULD HAVE I told her that she gone stay around when all this unfold with the feds.When she heard Congress offices calling me the Whitehouse and fbi agents and fbi prosecutor calling me about this murder plot upon me her hold attitude changed then it was all she ever been was good to me she ain't never did nothing to cross me YEA I BET...SHE said when this all over I will know that she rock with me I told her we will see time will tell. Same rule applies to any and all that took any part in this. Now let's get back to iron head after I bout the j30 I let Black see the car I send her a picture she the only person that i had sent a picture of the car to I call her in tell her I was coming to get my clothes.Because we stop fucking with each other about a week before she tell me to call in let her know when I'm on my way I tell her OK but I text her when I'm about 10 mins from her place. She know the way I come and leave it's only two ways to get to her place and from it. When I get off the freeway and get down the road a little I get pulled over the strange thing was this cop wanted to know where I was going I told him to get my clothes he ask a few more questions that had nothing to do with his supposed to be traffic stop it was bout the girl I'm going to see I just looked at him and didn't say nothing to him but you got my id and my paperwork he let me go.I get there and get my clothes and leave I get pulled over again only this police told me he just heard the other officer pull me over and he knows I'm legal.I ask then why would he pull me over he turned around walked half way to his truck and walked back to my car and told me i can leave and to hurry up and get back to Plano.The next night is when I go to Lancaster to go out to eat as soon as I exit the highway the law turns around and pull me over he impound my car and gives me no reason on why he impounding my car.I make it back the to the store the people iron head was with asking me have I seen him I tell them he left with y'all so iron head mommy pulls up asking if I had seen I told her who he was with she said he wasn't answering the phone.She said she went to the room but didn't no one answered i told her that I would go when I find a ride and told her I don't think she beat hard enough and I would have to do the same

.

A CHANGE HAS COME

Change

Rico events of his life exposes the corrupt illegal, Racketeering, genocide, government of America that can not be denied for all the world to see .This truth has brought a change to those that were still asleep.Every action gets a reaction Only the MOST HIGH GOD Can show the truth of his actions that YAHWEH IS THE MOST HIGH GOD AND HIS TRUTH CAN NOT go UNHEARD .. ULTIMATE BETRAYAL ....I get a ride to the room couple hours later and beat on the door iron head opens the door I tell him his mommy said she been calling him and he wasn't answering and told him she said she even came to the room.He look for his phone it's no where to be found he looks for his money and jewelry it's no where to be found I ask him who was the last person he was

with he tell me a gal he met that night SHE
ROBBED HIM FOR EVERYTHING HE HAD
WITH HIM MONEY PHONE BANK CARDS AND
ALL.I ASKED WHERE HE MEET HER AT HE
CANT REMEMBER I ASKED DO HE REMEM-
BER HOW SHE LOOK HE SAID HE DID AND
SAID SOMEBODY PUT THE BROAD ON TO
HIM.At this time he telling me about him and
drew getting into it and he feel like drew sent the
broad at him and started telling others times when
drew supposed to had stole from him and some
other shit he was telling me bout him and drew is-
sues.Time go passed he never found out who
ROBBED him. One night he claim his brother
them just made it in town I ask him from where
he tell me Louisiana they get there and it was two
of them so I'm asking them what part they from I
forget what part they claimed they was from but
one of them I knew his face.This was one that said
he wasn't from Shreveport but I knew his face and
told him so he got very uneasy few minutes pass
one of them go outside and come back in with a
40 cab with the beam on it now the one who said
he wasn't from Shreveport say he be in Shreveport all the time.I tell him that that's a nice 40 I
and say some other things and they was ready to

go at that point he realized I knew the game they was trying to run..A few days later I'm at the room iron head gone I hear iron head arguing with his mom like always but it was what was said that caught my attention.I hear iron head tell his mommy im going to do this and I want never have to worry bout money again in life.His mommy saying to him baby don't do that what the fuck is wrong with you he tells her he not try-ing to her any of that and he gone do it and that's it.He makes it to the door and comes in I'm sitting in the chair I asked him what him and his mom ar-guing about this time he replies something that's he gone do that he want have to worry about money ever again..About 48 hours pass by this time iron head gave me a key to the room I'm paying half on the room I go to the room with a lil broad iron head gone so I leaves the broad at the room for about 20 mins she text me and tells me please hurry up and get back because iron head tripping I asked her bout what she say he asking for pussy I laughed and said OK..I get there like 10 minutes after she text cause I was on the way back there when she text me.But I get there and I'm there for a few minutes I don't say anything to him bout what she just text me so he start talking off the wall ass shit till finally I asked what the fuck he talking about one thing led to another and now we arguing so I tell him are you mad cause you couldn't fuck her he get quite.Then say yea I asked for some pussy she in the room I laughed again and tell him so you mad cause you couldn't fuck her ..Now he slipped up and said something about the night I heard him and his mom arguing he called the laws on me and told the laws he wanted me out his room the laws asked had me and him and a fight he told them no then he told them I had weed told them what I was wearing and all the broad left me at the room everything was a plot from the start of it all..I left the room but not the building because my clothes was still in the room and I wasn't leaving without my shit that was simple.After the laws leave I go back in get my shit he opens the door I tell him he pussy for calling the laws and I said a few more things to him i rolled my blunt and got a ride down the street.At this time I got a warrant out for my arrest for the charge on Feb 10 2018 it's March my bond paid didn't have to pay again till April still no court date has been giving but, I got a warrant all illegal shit all because what I stand for.I find out about the warrant a few days after I leave the room but iron head already knew of this warrant this why he really called the police cause he knew about it because he was working with them against me..But I'm at another room down the street both a Month I get arrested let me explain.Im going to pay my phone bill one night the laws pull me over but as they pulling be over I pull into Walmart parking lot on Frankford and marsh lane.As I pull over I noticed this burgundy suburban with dark tint with government plates with fbi on the plates this like 2@ that morning this suburban almost come to a complete stop beside the sub I'm driving as if they trying to get a good look of who driving the suv. The suburban goes up a little and parks but no one gets out the lady officer notice I'm looking at this suburban and she o they just probably observing she runs my name I know for a fact I got this warrant cause I just talked to the sheriff the night before she comes back and gives me my id and a fake ticket only having my signature but not her name are badge number and tells me I can go.When I leave the suburban pull off behind me but it goes another way then I do.I get to the room and chill the next morning I go out a bounty Hunter comes out of the side of the building we have words but he never touch me cause he knows who I am and know I know my rights so the Dallas police get there run my name and say yes you have a warrant the night before it was a Dallas police officer that pulled me over.I go to jail to Dallas county then transferred to Denton county jail where the warrant is from.Denton county knows they have violated all kinds of FEDERAL and state law at this time Denton county has a FEDERAL lawsuit against them filed by me in Dallas Federal court the case is still open. Four months after I'm in jail I'm back out August 1 2018 I was free.On August 10 I get a call from my family in Shreveport telling me my lil COUSIN George Lee was killed shot multiple times two streets from where I was shot first thought came to my head was what he told me they wanted him to kill me and they was gone have to do what they had to because he love me and he not killing me I broke down knowing they killed my lil COUSIN and Shreveport police know exactly what for cause I told them a year before he was murdered Shreveport internal affairs Lt Greg Jackson his who I told before my family was murdered.Now it's time to apply PRESSURE but without the snakes knowing it I start with his sister who set it up making her feel as if we cool again until I get what is needed information so when it's time to sit with the Feds.The same as I did all other snakes played them at there on game letting them feel they was ahead but knowing they 10 steps behind.I eventually worked my way to every person and I didn't take long to do so. Once they figured out I know about it all they all started tell on each other Tonya fine told it on Tavara, Marcus ,Waco said he was gone make Sheba tell me what she told him because me Sheba and gc family and he gone make her tell me exactly what she told him but Tavara feared to get on the phone with me him and hear Why????? You see Tavara set it up and with me being alive and with what gc told me and all the recordings she knows it was a matter of time before this truth got out about the snake she is.Her killing our cousin Nikki was because Tavara failed to kill me when she poisoned me her setting her bro up was to spare her life because he didn't murder me it was him are her and she gave him to them when she the one who put all together even my bby mother Gladys Smith told me things like everything was coming from Tavara and GC.I will get to the recordings in the next chapter.The injustice system wins when one fear to stand up for what one knows is right the people are the only ones that can create change but first you must lose fear in order to stand for right. If one fear then one free to free themselves from the injustice that is forced on the ground of fear.Evil is strengthen by fear and fear is inflicted from those that wish to see are do evil one can not make it on knowledge alone and one can not make it on being fearless alone you must have both in order to stand cause without them both one will soon fall if both are not in tack with each other. Most of the time we fail only because we fear to try are because we fear we don't know enough to change if you fear to stand for what you know is right then you will submit to almost everything that you know is wrong. Only way to be a failure is to never try because you fear you will fail. Many say that they know what's wrong but yet those many fear to stand because they say you can't change it anyway.That comes from a person that fear what may happen to them for standing for what they know is right.Im use a great example 95 percent have sex but all know the good and bad of having sex but they go on with .Why is it different from standing up for what you know is right standing means you want settle for anything. A person will submit to man ways and want submit to God righteousness but will ask God to free them from man evilness in order to be free you must first not fear to stand for right. Life is a choice that we can make good are bad never the less it's your choice yes it is true that bad things happen to good people that don't mean you fear to stand because it may. When you stand for right you stand for GOD and when you stand for GOD YAHWEH things have to change a change has to COME. As I have stated many times NOTHING great come without risk many fear the risk so they never achieve greatness. One do not make one self great you are born great but you have to take the risk to reach are greatness and in order to take that risk you must truly trust the most high GOD who instill greatness in you before you was born faith without work is dead and to fear to be great is one on lack of trust to be free to truly live and live free. One must understand just because a person spend money on you are give you money are do anything for you that don't mean that person has your best interest in mind one must find the true agenda of why the person is doing what they are doing for them. If you are a person that thinks because someone does something for you that it means they care that's not always the case. The best way to keep someone around is to do for them it confuses the person that is being done for. People get love confused with money and tend to think that person love you are care about you never looking at the fact that it could be just to get you comfortable so they can proceed with their true agenda. It's many agendas a person could have so one must pay close attention to the person at hand.The secret society operate in secret moves so one has to be truly intact with the most high cause ONLY YAHWEH CAN LEAD ONE AND PROTECT YOU FROM THE EVIL YOU ARE BLIND TO THST EXIST. And the games and moves of those against you.You have to trust YAH-WEH in order for him to lead and guide you. To follow YAHWEH is not always a easy task, that's why he gives all a self choice. It's our self choice that determines how we live, it's that self choice that determines our greatness. If you have a child and your child don't believe you will protect them it's hard to protect them because the child want come for protection.One must seek the MOST HIGH GOD YAHWEH protection, his grace, his mercy, and his love, and peace!! God's love is un-deniable that many don't know but deceive the world as if the do. The greatest trick Satan ever pulled ,was to make the world believe he didn't exist, this is why so many can't see the evil darkness that has struck the world. The recordings from the fbi and many other agents prove this injustice of what I say and speak.

THE RESULTS TO IT ALL

Results

NoThe result of the actions from the corruption from within to destroy the Truly chosen one to lead THE MOST HIGH GOD PEOPLE.WAS THE strength that was needed to open the eye of the Last leader of the people to lead the people to truth to stand and reclaim what our GOD HAS GIVEN US ALL THINGS THAT WAS CREATED FOR ALL AND NOT JUST A FEW SELECTED.. This chapter will be short and to the point it just will give the agents of the recordings and names of those involved.The agents that confessed to the murder plot UPON my life is the united States general counsel office and USPTO The Dallas fbi has a court case saying Rico Cortez Dukes deceased after I filed a case with them the case was filed on July 31 2018 and on September 18 2018 it states I'm deceased but the case is still open.The documents from USPTO. The general counsel office told me I don't have to file a FEDERAL case because they can fix this matter I ask them do I suppose to over look the United States government tried to murder me they tell me no no we can fix this so you want have to file a FEDERAL case because they can fix this.I have many recordings with the fbi in regards to this matter Depository trust and clearing confessed I own the biotechnology account at Fidelity investments that's held at the Chicago Federal reserve Bank. Many Congress offices confess to many things from RACKETEERING to they have no jurisdiction over any American citizen the Whitehouse has contacted me about these matters as well even Congress offices have contacted me in regards to all this.The Louisiana Attorney general and the united States Marshall as I have stated in the early chapter of this book. I remember being in Shreveport and I asked YAHWEH what did he want me to do I cried in the bedroom I was in when I found out everything that I had found out I could not believe the same people that claim to love me was the very ones that wished me deceased.Wheather then to tell me they built in there heads that this could be done and they would live happy ever after with this being buried.When I spoke to my father that night in that room alone he told me you got to leave in order to put this together I asked where he gave the answer Texas I didn't know why it was Texas but I obeyed my father and went and my niece had her boyfriend pick me up on his way back from NEW Orleans.I had to stay in Shreveport to figure out what was going on and the key players and how they move and the games that they play and, the tricks that they use before God could send me to Texas.While still allowing me to find who I truly am a KING AND A LEADER. MANY FEMALES KEPT TELLING ME about a Jamie Prince Tamesha asked me Shirley asked me and Lasheka asked me that Tamesha and Sheba told me they was trying to see who he was cause he was pose to been going around giving woman hiv and said they trying to make sure they ain't fucked him are know him and I asked how did he look they described him as high yellow with freckles in his face but I had no clue who he was are had i ever seen him not knowing this was my lil bro pig close homeboy. This is also who my baby mother Shatory Washington told me about out of my 39 years on earth not one medical paperwork have ever said Rico Cortez Dukes was sick of any kind of hiv,cancer are anything other major health issue of any kind by the grace of the most high GOD YAHWEH and his son Yashua JESUS Christ. I want to discuss pistol and Daryl a little more in this chapter they are brothers that hung out at the store.They was from Mississippi are California I forget but anyway at a point when I started breaking away from Chrystal I started living at the brothers room at one time it was like six of us in one room like Mexicans.But never the less it worked. At this time I'm not knowing they rocking with Chrystal with the plot.I had a M1 with the 30 round clip and if one knows anything bout me I'm going to protect myself at all cost .While I'm at Daryl them room everyone got guns but mines the biggest and the baddest so I'm gone one night I'm at the store I get a call from Niño saying pistol said I can't keep my pistol at the room cause it's to big.Its only my gun that I'm being told that can't be there.So Niño ask do I need somewhere to keep it until I get straight I tell him yea I will get it back so I go pick him up and we go to his brother house to put it up a few days go by and I call him so we can go get it he tell me his brother wasn't home yet.I know this brother as well so I know he's always on the go. So I tell Niño to call his brother and let him know that we gone be by there when he get home. Couple days go by still nothing a few more days go by still nothing but me and Niño communicating thru out these days and he telling me the same as he was at first.So one day I'm hollering at another partner and I say something about my gun Niño got he tells me your gun a m1 30 round clip I said yea he said I know who got I said who he said cteez got it I said how he get he said Niño took over to cteez trying to sale but Niño owe cteez some money and cteez took it not knowing it was yours..Which I know cteez knew it was mines I finally get cteez and Niño together and asked them about it cteez admit he took it from Niño in front of Niño. I look at Niño and ask him how he gone try in clean up his debt with something that wasn't his..Weeks before this I was trying to sale it to C but he just fronted me without buying the gun he told me keep it I might need it just bring him the money from the front.So I tell Niño and cteez one of them gone have to pay me for my m1 cteez holla but Niño owe me Rico Niño holla cteez I paid you before I came with the gun I tell them I don't give a fuck who owe who all I know is my iron in the play of this and I'm not taking no lose on my shit that got nothing to do with you and Niño debt and told them I'ma get my money one way are the other. About a week are so later cteez put a zip in a half in my hands cause he was about to go out of town yep I kept the weed after that I had got cteez gun 9mm for iron head cteez thought I was gone bring it because he knew the play they did but I had the green so I was cool on his end.He called me a million times saying come on Rico I need it man.A day are two went by before I took it back to him and told him you thought I was gone not bring it to you.About a week after that Niño give me 30 x pills yep I keep now both debts are clean with me so I'm cool. Remember I said me and the female I call Black was living together at that time she took me to take the gun back to him she knew very well of what was going on with me and them I made sure I told her. Chrystal plan was to get me dis armed for the plot can roll smooth pistol them job was to dearm me for the plot but they had to figure out how to do it so they waited and came with a bullshit plan well I guess the plan worked cause it got the m1.Through it all I have with stood many test and after putting all this truth out the feds waiting for me to come sit down with the Federal agent and Federal prosecutor about this murder plot that comes from there very own people.This book is the proof and understanding for the feds along with the audio recordings.Yes America I'm handing those that took part in this plot back to they boss they made the deals with.Instead of the hunter they became the hunted YAHWEH works in ways the human flesh mind can not understand. One must understand his are herself first before one can began to comprehend the works of GOD. Many fear to be who they are destined to be for fear of what the world might say are think. Somewhere along the line we forgot how to stand without fear but we stand without fear against one other for the ones that oppress us. We fear to use our minds to free ourselves so how can we fault this who oppress us we must first fault ourselves for the lack of knowledge we choose not to seek.We can only be oppressed from lack of knowledge I'm going to explain something music acting modeling etc is cool how many people that rappers singers actors etc you she at the end that came with nothing they leave with nothing because they lack the knowledge to understand how to keep up with the money they was making and spending.My point is we spend our lives depending on someone to keep up with our things that at the end everyone has your things but you.Lets take the IRS for example many have no clue that tax is ILLEGAL many may say how? Pbnba irs code 1.001-1 4657cch tells you that all FEDERAL reserve note dollars are value-less and ILLEGAL and unlawful. One must ask they self if money is ILLEGAL then how can tax be legal it's no way possible.How is it the irs can come take your property and it's paid off. The game is this how can you own something that was paid with something that was ILLEGAL from the start this the same as a drug dealer property being seized because the property was bought with ille-gal drug money the irs knows this but the sleeping people don't know this and they fear this along with many other things to be known and acted upon. Responsible lies with the American people to stand and change the corruption from those we put in power TO PROTECT US FROM ANY FORM OF CRIME BUT THEY HAVE FAILED TO INCLUD THEMSELVES to be prosecutor so they prosecutor the people for lack of knowledge and lack of courage to stand for what they know is right. We must stand as one in order to see change that we cry for we much teach and speak without fear of what might happen. We must abandon the thought of just bout our on individual family and think of all families that are being oppressed. This is the only way we can ever see true change to rededicate ourselves with truth and not lies strengthen ourself with courage and stand no matter how high the stakes.Nothing great comes without great risk.

THE VOICE FOR THE PEOPLE

People voice

Rico never knew he would become the voice for the people never knowing the power that come with the voice of truth that stand for the people .... Standing for the people come with great responsibility and great risk and great rewards for those he are she stands for.Only the chosen can and will stand no matter how high the stakes this is the closing chapter of my book.The voice for the people can not fear the evil that lurks from within its own GOVERNMENT. The voice for the people must be able to tell there fault as well as show there good never forgetting he are she is human to. The voice of the people must educate those he are she stand for The voice must not be confused on who they serve meaning the most high GOD YAHWEH.A voice is something that is felt by those you have never seen are talked to but they have heard your voice and feel the truth of power behind it that can not be denied. To be the voice one can not be afraid to fail because it will be many set backs within your journey only those that are chosen to be a voice will and can rise above every set back that comes before them.To lead one must understand his are her facing death threats for the truth that they choose to stand for. Only the chosen can withstand this ULTIMATE task the fact of knowing you could be hurt are killed for standing for those that are blind history as showed us this many many times.I have a great journey ahead of me that has just begun for the world to see the events in my life was meant for all to see the power of what the most high can bring your through and take you to.I remember Trigger told me Rico a nigga holding your ace card so what I'm going to do about it.When all this came together I asked was the ace card still being held he replied no and told me now you know now what you gone do about it I replied just wait and see he got very quite upon my reply to him. The God I serve said he will make your enemies your foot stool MY GOD NEVER LIES..The name of those that MY GOD LEAD me TO WAS VERY

MANY CLOSE FAMILY AND FRIENDS with undeniable facts and proof.I had to learn that every word my father speaks is 1 TRILLION Percent true and will never change..HE TOLD US NEVER TRUST YOUR MOTHER YOUR FATHER YOUR SISTER BECAUSE THEY WILL FORSAKE YOU BUT I WILL NEVER FORSAKE YOU...IM A LIVING TESTIMONY WITH 23 GUNSHOT HOLES TO SHOW WITH DOCUMENTS AFTER DOCUMENTS OF UNBEARABLE FACTS THAT CAN NOT BE DENIED..I AM RICO CORTRZ DUKES ...THE SON OF YAHWEH ...KING AND LEADER....AND SON OF THE KING OF KINGS... YAHWEH AND HIS SON JESUS CHRIST YASHUA....WITHOUT HIM THERE IS NO ME ... WITHOUT HIM THERE IS NO US...It's much to come from with this book ULTIMATE FAMILY BETRAYAL....TO BE CONTINUED

[1] ONE CAN ONLY HAVE FAILURE ONLY IF ONE FEAR TO FAIL

[2] This book is dictated in loving memory of my Little cousin (GC)GEORGE CALVIN LEE JR.WHO WAS MURDERED FOR NOT MURDERING ME ..HIS NAME SHALL LIVE THROUGH ME RICO, HIS BIG COUSIN I WILL NEVER FORGET HIS WORDS TO ME ..REST IN PEACE FAM..WORDS CAN NOT DESCRIBE MY HURT..

[3] This book is from inspiration of the events YAHWEH AND HIS son Yashua JESUS Christ has brought me through and bringing me through. It is by his grace and mercy I'm allowed to write this book for all the world to see and learn.. Yahweh is the ULTIMATE GOD AND THE ONLY CREATOR OF ALL THINGS HE HIS LOVE....

www.ingramcontent.com/pod-product-compliance
Lightning Source LLC
LaVergne TN
LVHW090158180726
843489LV00006B/2108